HARVESTING FOG

Also by Luci Shaw

POETRY

Listen to the Green

The Secret Trees

Postcard from the Shore

Polishing the Petoskey Stone

Writing the River

The Angles of Light

The Green Earth

Waterlines

What the Light Was Like

FOR CHILDREN

The Genesis of It All

MUSICAL SCORES

Alice Parker

Alan Cline

Frederick Frahm

Knut Nystedt

Roland Fudge

Ed Henderson

ANTHOLOGIES

Sightseers into Pilgrims

A Widening Light

Accompanied by Angels

WITH MADELEINE L'ENGLE

Wintersong

A Prayer Book for Spiritual Friends

Friends for the Journey

FESTSCHRIFT

The Swiftly Tilting Worlds of Madeleine L'Engle

PROSE

God in the Dark

Water My Soul

The Crime of Living Cautiously

Breath for the Bones

Harvesting Fog

poems

Luci Shaw

PINYON PUBLISHING

Montrose, Colorado

Front cover photograph copyright © 2010 by Susan Elliott
Back cover photograph copyright © 2010 by John Hoyte

First Edition: 2010

Pinyon Publishing
23847 V66 Trail, Montrose, CO 81403
www.pinyon-publishing.com

Library of Congress Control Number: 2009944213
ISBN: 978-0-9821561-2-4

Acknowledgements

Heart- and mind-felt thanks to friends who have heard and read my poems and helped me discover where the poems wanted to go. I'm thinking of Tim Anderson, Jennifer Bullis, Karen Cooper, Carol Lichtenberg, Mike Mason, Ron Reed, John Shaw, and Jeanne Murray Walker.

Special thanks to Scott Cairns for his careful reading of the entire manuscript.

I am grateful to the editors of the following publications in which these poems first appeared, some in a slightly different form or with a title change, for permission to reprint the poems in this book:

Books & Culture: "The chair without distinction," "The Two of Them," "O"

Basilica: "Cedar Ghost"

Christian Century: "Lightening," "Now! Order your prepaid cremation!"

Christianity & Literature: "Canaan Valley, October," "The Buildings of Languedoc, France"

Crux: "Kenosis"

El Porvenir: "The Songs of Camoapa"

Image: "Psalm for the January Thaw"

The Living Church: "The Returns of Love"

Nimble Spirit (online): "Indeterminacy," "Being," "Gardener's Remorse"

The Other Journal (online): "A Few Suggestions for an Insubordinate Idea"

Radix: "Walkway"

Relief: "Consider"

Rock & Sling: "Stephansdom Cathedral, Vienna, " "Dilemma"

Ruminate: "I say light, thinking," "Overhead"

Spirituality & Health: "Forgiveness"

The Southern Review: "Caunes, Minervois"

Vineyards: "Campground, California Coast," "On retreat," "Hearth fire"

Weavings: "Watcher," "Reconstruction"

for

Greg & Suzanne Wolfe

contents

fog

a fore word

I was transfixed several months ago, while reading the *National Geographic*, to discover that in Lima, Peru, a coastal city where there is very little rain but a persistent clammy fog due to the high humidity, the locals hang rags and nets on clotheslines and balconies until they're saturated with moisture from the mist. They wring the cloths out for the water they've collected. They do this again and again, all year long. It's a means of survival. They call it "harvesting fog."

Aha, I thought. That's a lot like writing poems. Something's in the air, a word, an impression, a rhythmic phrase, a sound, a small connection. You grab it and then you catch more drops and pool them altogether, and wring some fresh meaning out of them, and as if by miracle this mystery, this moisture becomes a new entity that satisfies a thirsty imagination. Sometimes, in the process, the words themselves tell you where they want to go, as if they too were thirsty to find their meaning in a universe full of possibilities.

We use the word "wonder" often, and too casually. Yet it is what we hunger for, and recognize when history, or the every-day, is transformed into something we try to pin down, to capture, and hold. Sometimes only poetry can fasten it there, pinned on a page or spoken into air so that the wonder echoes and re-echoes, enlivening our sense of the unseen, barely translatable real. The O.T. prophets had to do this, suddenly burdened with visions like dreams (think Ezekiel), with a foot in two worlds, required to transmit the message to the people in a time of conflict, corruption, or celebration.

Abstractions and generalizations like "conflict," or "corruption," seldom work to enliven the mind. We need specifics like a color, a story, an event, a texture to bring them home to us. This is where the detail of poetry and fiction can be revelatory, and this is where the role of the writer as a kind of "translator" is vital.

Such harvesting is something that happens when the mind is open to possibility. Its outstanding feature is its availability to the imagination. I'm sometimes asked how a poem happens for me. All I can say is that it's a magical thing, difficult to explain or describe. Like me, many artists struggle to define their creative process in terms that are clear for others. The impulse can happen in an instant, unpremeditated, usually triggered by something quite ordinary and earthy—some trick of light, someone else's compelling work of art, some weather condition, the furled shape of a cloud or a hill, the color of a leaf—a close-up detail like the lattice of a spider web, or an intellectual concept that is amenable to metaphor.

The process involves paying attention, being willing to investigate and allow the image to gain in intensity and significance. I get hooked by an idea the way a fish gets hooked out of its normal fluid habitat or, more appropriate to the idea of the transcendent, the way an insect is snagged from the air in a net. Maybe a casual conversation moves my thought in a new direction. It's as if some transcendent transaction lies in wait for me to recognize it, pluck it out of this other world, and begin to record it. It comes with a sense of availability, of given-ness, and a generosity that enlarges my understanding of the cosmos. "Transported" is a word that comes to mind. I love what Dorothy Sayers said, on completing a novel: "I feel like God on the Seventh Day!"

The whole thing partakes of mystery. Poets can sometimes sense that they have a foot in both the concrete, visible world and the ephemeral, invisible world, translating the experience of a spiritual realm into word pictures in order to bring a whiff of heaven to earth. This happens all too rarely, but often enough to augment our sense of truth's availability, of linking the many dimensions of the universe.

Then before they've evaporated, words are jotted onto a journal page or directly into the computer. Then comes the work, the craft, the listening for the musical and rhythmic line, the shape-shifting of metaphors, getting the tone and color right, searching for the authentic startling word or resonant phrase to be worked into the fabric of the writing. I love having a glowing computer screen to work with, moving morsels of type around, experimenting, deleting, paring down to an essence. "Maybe this stanza should come first." "This sounds too somber; it needs a bit of mischief." "OK, I love this bit, but it has to go. Maybe it's part of another poem." "Hmmm. I like the friction going on with these consonants." Until, many drafts later, it has found its final form and feels complete, like a box closing with a click, as Robert Frost noted.

The harvesting equipment a writer needs is minimal, like the Peruvian rags—something to write with or write on—beyond that, an open, curious mind, a habit of fielding questions that don't necessarily have answers, combing the ether for information or disclosure. That's where the idea of fog gives me hope—all those damp little particles waiting to be collected into water for cleansing, for thirst.

As for you, reader, give these poems time to gather, let them soak in.

—Luci Shaw, Bellingham, 2009

It is only by selection, by elimination, by emphasis
that we get at the real meaning of things.
—*Georgia O'Keeffe*

harvest

PRISM

Through window glass the sun crosses my shoulder,
condensing into a small rainbow beetle.
He creeps along a line of type on the left page of
my novel, with its description of the protagonist's

facial expression. What, minutes ago, was
an adjective in a field of violet is now suffused
with yellow verging on neon green,
dyes so intense they stain my thumbnail,

turn mere knots of letters into signal flares.
Now the beetle is bridging the book's
gutter to tour the facing page across a patch
of dialog and, curious about what comes next,

prepares to tumble its radiance off the far right
edge of the paper onto my wrist bone.
I welcome you, small envoy of colored light,
as you begin to write your own story on my skin.

I SAY LIGHT, THINKING

I say *light,* thinking, gift—
the color of the street lamp
from where I sit—and the word *golden*
edges into my mouth. My lips
part and close again over it, like taking in
something as solid as a bite of
butter, so real it melts.

               And when light
comes from nowhere I can see,
when my soul is clothed in
golden bandages, ribbons of grace,
how can I tell you? Or even tell myself
so I can write it down? No words
are bright enough to catch
those fingerprints of radiance
that flicker on my wall.

CONSIDER

(sidereal, of or pertaining to the stars)

Glass can never be thin enough
to translate out from in, unaltered.
I open every window to entice air
and with it the landscape—its dark bulk.

A peep shot (through a squared frame
of thumbs and fingers). Only a tittle
of indigo, barely a jot of enormity,
but some kind of edge shatters out there
and in here. And speaking of stars,
the word *desire* itself. The sky a whole,
filling the hole of the heart.

RECONSTRUCTION

Sometimes, like an Andy Goldsworthy
assemblage, You take us to the very edge
of our collapse. And when it happens,
and the ice is eaten away by its own melting,
and wind takes the straws, there You are,
ready to rebuild with endless patience.

You splint the cracked bones, tether
the shaky spirits. Even as it crumples
You plan the rebuilding of the body, readying it
for new resilience, a shape that brings You
pleasure, lets You sit back, exuberant,
"That's it. Hold it right there! Breathe."

OBEDIENCE

When my fingers
know better than I
as they hover over
the keyboard, then type
a word that is not
the word I wanted but
a better word—what is that
but an answer. You
caring for details, filling
cracks, your tongue
arc-ing its swift current
through my bones.

PSALM FOR THE JANUARY THAW

1.

Blessed be God for thaw, for the clear drops
that fall, one by one, like clocks ticking, from
the icicles along the eaves. For shift and shrinkage,
including the soggy gray mess on the deck
like an abandoned mattress that has
lost its inner spring. For the gurgle
of gutters, for snow melting underfoot when I
step off the porch. For slush. For the glisten
on the sidewalk that only wets the foot sole
and doesn't send me slithering. Everything
is alert to this melting, the slow flow of it,
the declaration of intent, the liquidation.

2.

Glory be to God for changes. For bulbs
breaking the darkness with their green beaks.
For moles and moths and velvet green moss
waiting to fill the driveway cracks. For the way
the sun pierces the window minutes earlier each day.
For earthquakes and tectonic plates—earth's bump
and grind—and new mountains pushing up
like teeth in a one-year-old. For melodrama—
lightning on the sky stage, and the burst of applause

that follows. Praise him for day and night, and light
switches by the door. For seasons, for cycles
and bicycles, for whales and waterspouts,
for watersheds and waterfalls and waking
and the letter *W,* for the waxing and waning
of weather so that we never get complacent. For all
the world, and for the way it twirls on its axis
like an exotic dancer. For the north pole and the
south pole and the equator and everything between.

WEIGHT LOSS

That bones will brittle
Is my truth,
And that all little
Cells, forsooth,

Will fail and fall,
And falling, leave
My brain's recall.
So I receive

Lightness of being,
And a beginning
Of agreeing
With this thinning.

So long, lucidity.
Welcome, life's
Gentle finality—
Its gradual knife.

Forgive the cells
That float and fly.
They've done quite well,
And so have I.

THE RETURNS OF LOVE
after George Herbert

There is such generosity in love it will not fit
Within a modest box with corners and a key.
But what if I offer more than I receive? If
My love's largesse, though open, unencumbered, free,
And furnished without stint to all my friends and foes,
Vanishes in the void, is spent, and lost to me?

Then I remember—love, not cramped in where it goes,
May be reversed, enlarged by love's complicity,
Its give and take. The sumptuous fragrance of a rose
Accepts no close confinement or captivity.
The tide that outward ebbs, turns then and inward flows,
And what I offer you, you'll multiply to me.

RECOGNITION

Who on earth saw him first, knowing
surely who he was? Belly to belly, when
John, prophet in utero, distinguished
in the natal soup the fetal bones, the body
curled like a comma, eyes tight, skull
packed with universal wisdom,
this unborn cousin began to dance.

And when she, birth-giver—
her ordinary vision arrowed down between
her legs, through pain and straw, to her son's dark,
slime-streaked hair, to his very skin, red with
the struggle of being born—she lifted him
to her breast, kissed the face of God,
and felt her own heart leap.

THEN AND NOW

Night wind on the cheek.
In the air a sliver of song, "born today."
An ancient story, told so often, for so long
it feels remote. I need to live my lack, to feel
three or more dimensions, shivers
of color, of cold—thick dark, with a whiff
of straw, and maybe a winter star
through a doorway.

All at once
I'm there, lifting the new one
in my arms, this small sack of God
slung safe in my elbow's crook,
comfort warm as blood seeping
through the swaddle. I kiss
the wet red face, eyes bright
as a tiny bird's, and I nearly burst—as if
I'm ready myself to give birth—
with the heart surge that tells me
it really happened, is happening,
is more actual than any crèche
fronting any church.

MASSAGE

He comforts me with blankets,
compresses the bellows of my torso with
both hands, telling the lungs Let out
the old air. Welcome fresh. His touch
turns multiple as he circles,
assuring each body part his full attention—
his plan to teach each one mercy,
restoration. Then the work begins,
strong, fluid, repetitive as water.
I melt as I am mended.

Face down, I'm blind and he invisible.
I sense him bending, moving silently
around me as I lie on my soft altar. Now and then,
through the face-cradle, I see the flash of feet
as he anoints me, length and limb.

Trust gives me freedom to let go,
to let my body listen without speaking, to know
I'm safe. The foot bones, muscles, shoulder tendons
recognize his fingers. He tells me that
my dogwood flower tattoo is to his liking.
He knows my body better than I do myself—
knows the neck-knots, the joints where pain
has built its citadel, which he demolishes.
When he's done he tells me, Take your time
before you move. And water is good. Lots of water.

A FEW SUGGESTIONS FOR
AN INSUBORDINATE IDEA

You've untangled yourself from my hair,
floating behind me on one very thin strand.

So I loose you to the early air, not wanting teething
or sleepless nights, hoping you'll find your way

at a young age. So, little enthusiast, full
of possibilities, don't die. Photosynthesize.

Grow your own green leaf, or several. Bleed
oxygen for my breathing. Absorb my CO_2.

Together we may balance the atmosphere.
Drop a seed into the humus of old thoughts.

Offer a nipple for a neighbor's thirst
or a flake of desert manna with a honey sweetness.

Oh, small particulate of the mind, why not
turn to lightning in a bug that signals: Stop. Go.

Start a blaze hot as a fatwood fire. Fling
a glitter of ash over the ocean, pocking it like rain.

Ignite a burning bush. Transfix the universe. Then,
having found a mind of your own, come home.

Burrow my brain. Be one of a neuron couplet
that breeds a host of your own kind.

THE CHAIR WITHOUT DISTINCTION

This, in praise of inanimate objects,
of the offering I brought home last year
from the church rummage sale.
A useful color in basic fabric,
a button missing among its worn tufts.
Sturdy, not graceful. Dependable,
not particularly easy. In a corner of
the room, out of the way, people sit on it
when the space gets crowded. They chat
with friends, coffee cups in hand,
then rise and move on without
noticing. Why should they notice?

WIND AND WINDOW

No snow, but the sleet
tapping loud on the skylight,
like stars wanting entrance.
A message keeps coming—
wind humming a tune
in the branches of cedars,
a rumor of heaven,
a whisper of God:
No snow, but a sound
penetrating your window.
You can't see the gusts
but listen, and sense me—
I'm the spice in the air,
the cool on your cheek,
a shift of the season,
a change in your weather.
Swing wide your window,
to hear what I'm saying,
like Mary who listened,
her heart thrown ajar.

WATCHERS

Behold the fleck of ant
bearing with diligence his large
load of crumb down the long
mile of floorboard.

If, by observation, we become
part of an insect's life, is he
aware of us? What thread of vision
links antic and observant?
What false criterion of size?
And who is it who, watching us,
whispers Watch for Who it is
Who watches you?

FORGIVENESS

This morning's fall of white lends the rough sedge
a fresh perfection (much as powder on a face
will hide a rash), and lays on roof and ledge
this tablecloth, covering every trace

of wounded earth. Old injury is now erased,
as wood and mossy tile and road and bridge
are evened out with flakes as fine as lace
on which each footprint seems a sacrilege.

Even the tire tracks across the bridge
are filling with new white that will embrace
the contrasts between muddy groove and ridge,
like contrarieties within the human race.

Earth's sores and blemishes are each erased,
under the kind gauze of bandages—
dressings that high heaven has cleanly placed
over the roughened roadside foliage,

healing the raggedness of grass and hedge.
This patient snow refreshes morning's face,
forgives shortcomings, rounding every edge,
a blessing looking very much like Grace.

PHOTOS FROM MY TRIP

Inching out of the printer, here come
the slits of color that reveal a field in Devon
blazing like green fire, and a thatched cottage
and a couple of sheep and a horse. And Bath,
and gargoyles grinning from a pillared bas-relief.
Here comes Clovelly; tangled turquoise fishnets
drying on the rocks. And here's my husband sketching
and the tide behind him pushing into
the narrow harbor, lifting the boats from the mud
almost as fast as this print is pulsing out of
the machine's mouth. Here comes the day
rising over Glastonbury Tor, and the abbey
un-restored, a mouth gaping at heaven.
Here's Bibury and its swans and the stream full of
the shapes of dark trout. Here come the clouds,
and then a blurred photo with rain on the lens.

Now it's Exeter Cathedral and a late sun
burning red through a glassy Jesus onto my hand,
the hand that receives him now, urged out
bit by bit like a baby from the womb, on a blank
sheet of photo paper with colored ink
from a cartridge I bought at the store.

THE VOICE IN THE PINES
National Forest Service Campground, Pend-d'Oreille, Washington

The pine-tops start to stir, to sway their pencil trunks
and waken the soft sound of breath—silk on sadness.
Even listening in the tent, a distance opens, asking:
How does air make music? Does it seek
a solid thing to rub against and send a sigh that is a song,
a long continuo of song that plays a hillside like a harp?

It asks me now to catch this freshness in a bucket,
haul it in to do its work on me (though it might die
and all its gusts be gone), then free it to the larger air until
it moves, and then moves on, lifting me with it.

RECIPE FOR CONCRETE
Lomas de Cafen, Nicaragua, for El Porvenir

You need sand, so you begin to pour the dug-up
heap of dirt through a sieve made with old
wire screening tacked to a wood frame, sifting it
by the half bucketful, watching it rise into
its own little hill, there between the ragged
banana palms. This feels like breaking down
your own humanity into manageable dust.

You find a shovel, then, rusty, looking as beat up
as you are in the hot sun, and you spade
the six buckets of sand you need for concrete into
a new pile, heaving it and mixing it with three measures
of the gravel. You scoop and lift and turn, scoop and lift
and turn. From the truck bed Antonio has just unloaded
a cement sack, a pale weight that sags in the middle

on the man's shoulder as he carries it, a magical offering
for bonding the sand with gravel, the way both unity
and discrepancy bind rough with refined, body with spirit.
It is two miles to the river, but in blue plastic barrels
water is at hand, drawn from the new well. Mortar
needs juice as badly as lungs need breath, so in your
small volcano you open a caldera to pour the water into.

There's an odd sense that you are working with hands
larger than your own as you shovel the grainy edges of
the solids into the middle, and the water sinks in. Careful.
Don't waste the precious fluid in a trickle to the ground.
Keep swelling the mix with water; the more you sprinkle into
the little crater lake, the weightier, until you can trust its
consistency. Pour it by the bucketful into the prepared form,

nudge it into corners with a hand trowel. Finally, level it with
a straight board. This will be the foundation for the wash tubs
and shower stalls beside the well. It must cure and harden
for fifteen days, long enough to keep it from cracking. There
the women will come with their dusty feet, and their washing,
no longer needing to walk to the river. Pray they will
know that this lavandero is a temple for the Holy Ghost.

THE SONGS OF CAMOAPA

Deep dusk, and the thin moon pleads Look up, look up.
A salting of stars whispers with their white Wink, wink.
Vroom, vroom roars the ancient taxi up the cobbled hill.
Sweet, sweet, sobs the bird in the mango tree.

Yowl, yowl, gripes the bony cat in the midnight alley.
Cock-a-roo-roo declares the rooster on the hill.
The breakfast plantains in the fry pan spatter Spit, spit.
Sweet, sweet, cries the bird in the mango tree.

Lurch, lurch, sways the truck up to the work site.
The saw bites the plank in two directions—Ta-co, Ta-co.
The hammers on the nails pound Pom-pom, Pom-pom.
Sweet, sweet, calls the bird in the mango tree.

Crunch, crunch, mutters my shovel heaving gravel,
Then swish, swish, as the water makes cement.
Rattle, rattle, rattle, whisper wind-dried palm fronds.
Sweet, sweet, laughs the bird in the mango tree.

Hola! Hola! shout the children of Lomas de Cafen,
Water from the new well gushes Drink! Drink!
Gracias! Gracias! cry the women with their washing.
Sweet, sweet, trills the bird in the mango tree.

LITURGY, NOOKSACK RIVER, NORTH FORK

Under the bank a trouble of water
foams where boulders interrupt the rush
of milk-pale river. Furious stones
kicking back. A bubble and rattle, a protest
of submerged pebbles. And at the edges
—marginalia to a fluid text—scribbles of gravel
fractured to anonymity among skeletal roots
cry pardon for their frailty,
their failure to survive the current.

The weep of snow, of folded blue glacier
melting under the mountain's lap, sweeps clean
the mineral bed. Something sacramental speaks
in the rinsing of hard stone by mountain run-off
that pours, like a solvent, in and out of season,
teaching me what humility feels like,
and the fierce mercy of absolution.

OVERHEAD

The sun is a slow gong
in a brass bowl, the moon also

rings her bell against
the indigo steel of the night sky.

By painting, Emily Carr
decoded heaven as coastline

vast bays of ripped blue
and Vincent drew his circles

tighter than the tattered orbits
of his own life.

Art like that
irrational and entire

is all perception
the surreal turning real:

how poets sift what they see
into what they feel,

pulling new pieces of heaven
into view.

ON RETREAT
New Camaldoli Hermitage, Big Sur

This early morning, in the chill before light,
I lie open, face upward on the little bed,
a supplicant, body reflecting soul, ready
for something I cannot see, but crave.

I'm waiting, like any fern in a garden,
to be rained on, or sun-drenched.

Oh, I am little, little.

The day lifts its face over the Pacific
and a corner of sun touches the thin pillow.
I shift my head under its warm hand;
it moves across my face as I lie quite still.
It blesses my forehead with its holy oil.

What is blessing but a largeness
so immense it crowds out
everything but itself?

HOLDING ON

Seven days since the storm
snowed itself out and moved east, and still
the fat clots of white lodge themselves
in the twig forks, held up to be noticed
by the world. How cold holds!
This snow fruit crotched in place
by the black dogwood, snared by
a relentless frost that won't
let go, won't give in, even to the sun.
I fixed it in my camera's eye.

On my dining table, in a wood
bowl, wait the five dried pomegranates
I've saved for a friend. Decay has
forgotten them, their red skin
dried to tough brown leather,
the little teeth of sepals crimped
in a crown of sharp kisses that guard
the secret seeds, dark purses
for a blood that will never spill.

FRIO RIVER, TEXAS

The river, up to the ankles,
invites our feet to test its depth and learn
through the skin of our soles
how water chisels limestone,
knuckling it, leaving the long print of fluid
all along the stream bed. We discover

what it might be like to walk on water,
and how the stone supports the flow
composing its own fluid music, a naked sound
around us as we wade, a lilt that lightens the heart.
Together, sun and stone and water write
their rippling continuo between the hills.
Sometimes the lens of water, like an eye,
deepens to a blue profundity, the way
music needs no words, being
its own language. Its own measure.

EVENING, COOLING

We step out the door, measuring the way
we move into the garden. Paper thin,
shadows pool their long shapes across
the sidewalk. We walk into them as they
stretch before us, our dark companions.
As light drowns itself behind the hill, an eyelid
closing, our skin notices the cool. Day lilies nod.
Succulents turn from violet and jade to the color
of dust. Deepness grows in the ravine.
Our green hands drop to our sides.

We have been shaped all day by heat
and blaze, and hammers echoing
from skeletal houses. Summer is a kiln,
and with evening, under the hardening clay,
new colors begin to show themselves
beneath the glaze. Parched from the sweet fever
of the season, dust settles grain by grain
as the lake breathes. Venus appears, and other
bright bodies. Our talk dies as we surrender
our voices to the air. Listen.
Except for one, all the birds hush.

GARDENER'S REMORSE

I have always welcomed the perennials
but today I celebrate weeds. The arrival of
horse-tails, their primitive vigor thrusting up
under the fence as if the Third Day of Creation

were just yesterday. In penance, as redemption,
I will begin to touch the earth more lightly.
remembering to walk barefoot in the soft
forest so that I make no bruit nor break,

and where the concrete cracks I will let
the slow velvet of green gather in the concrete
cracks. Without resentment I'll allow every
varied herb to assert itself again, crowding in,

confident, sifting its secret seeds under lavender,
heather, cotoneaster. Cedar seedlings prickle
from the earth, hoping to start a small forest;
it could bring shade for our house. I will treasure

the gold exuberance of buttercups and the generous,
feathery legacy of ageing dandelions.
I notice the mole's dark castings, mottling the grass,
hidden from their lowly earth-movers. From the path

I will applaud their diligent constructions and refrain
from trampling them in anger. And the deer
stalking up from the creek—buck and doe—
clipping tulips so that only brief stalks poke

from the soil—they are fully forgiven. As I fight
second thoughts, I notice the slugs' rainbow slime
on the paving stones and the crusts of jade aphids
on the lupines. Determined, I resolve to regard them

as adornments. As for the gravel, the pale
pebbles that have surfaced through soil,
through time, I will leave their small bony faces
to stare me down, so that I will not forget.

DILEMMA

Determined to leave words behind (rubbing me raw
from every inside surface—my deeply-papered desk,
the spines of the books on the shelves, the magazines
exploding with syllables, the verbal assault of the cereal box
on the counter, even the apples' stuck-on labels)
I open my window over the ravine. The flowing creek with
its splash and hush. A deep breath. The intake—a lovely
wet, fungal smell. A squirrel's sharp decrescendo
of chirrup. So promising, but not enough.

When the front door swings wide the world
pulls me out, a cork from a bottle, to where
the only words come as wind empties its bowlful
of cool in my face. The clouds speak a drench of rain.
A wide bib of creek water over rocks repeats, over
and over, its original haiku. The sun comes out,
articulating its meaning on a pool. It all begins to become
enough, even the bird, in its purse of a nest, brooding,
not singing. Even silence a sweet, pure language.

DECEMBER

A forty-eight hour fall with more to come.
Our life suspended. The flakes, heavy and

discrete, rise on roof and rail to loaves of snow.
The generous sky breeds a pearly light

with no shadow. We up the heat against
the forecast's drop. Voices on the phone agree,

It's beautifully dangerous. Stay home.
Somewhere the repeated, muted sound—

a shovel shifting from a sidewalk
its soft, square load.

CANAAN VALLEY, OCTOBER

We've come to expect it from trees, but here
even the ground blazes, packed deep with leaf foil
red as red gold. At every turn in the road
we're jolted by another roar of color—whole hillsides
belting out the flush the sun has invested
in West Virginia foliage all last summer.

I'm hearing a story from 1910. Settlers, determined
to clear the land, cut down every tree along
the mountain's backbone. They had themselves pictured,
triumphant, standing on stumps. When
the exposed leaf-peat caught fire it burned away,
burned clear down to the limestone bones of the hills.

This morning the defiant blaze of fallen leaf on every side
campaigns for revival. No cautious pigment,
just the bright brush of a view through the car window
that sweeps all the old years' records clean.
A flame that refuses to go out,
to join the lost history of leaves.

Oceans may muddle salt with fresh so that
sources are forgotten. Glass cannot tell you
from which of millions of sand grains it has been melted
and cooled to clarity. But mountains are made

of memory, eons of it, an ancient narrative held tight
in the rocks; their deep hum of survival a sostenuto
all winter, inaudible to us. But come spring, we'll know
to watch for a green fire singing along the hills again.

CEDAR GHOST

Quite often I watch for a cedar to sway,
to signal a fresh breath—listening for a voice like
the rush of a flume, a word soft as feathers of air

in June, a steady draft that carries
cottonwood seeds past the window, like soft refugees,
or emissaries of peace, or undercover agents,

as well as the keen wind that hurls leaves,
and then snow, the wind that dies
and resurrects before it speaks again.

The branches translate the fingers
of invisible air into movement, an insurrection,
an evidence of the unseen,

but how to attempt a likeness with words
for wind, for how it flings and sings, how it
comes to rest after the work is done?

I see wind as essence of heaven.
The jay on the high branch sees it green,
a silk, a sheer scarf for the planet.

Now wind's own words are taking flight, arriving
from seven distances of hills, with hints of salt,
of fog. Of wood smoke blue as opals.

Dust particles from the Gobi. Of rain finding
a perch in our branches, settling there like moths
or migratory warblers, until time is up.

THE GENEROSITY OF PINES

There must still be a life in the wood even after
months stacked in the pile in the yard, open-hearted
host to spiders and small rodents, the blunt ends jutting,
else how could the flames leap so high, so lively
from the logs? As if all their piney essence
is gathering itself in one final declaration, yielding
its being to us—we, hunkered around its comfort,
warming our hands, our faces grateful.

It burns as if to reassure itself of merit, of true
timber. As if to let us know that the long years
of achieving dense and muscular and tall
could be summed up in these joyous needles
and cones of flame, and the vitality of resin spit and split.
As if flinging its fervor through the air in the room
is a special aptitude—even the coals, pulsing
with red heat, emitting threads of smoke
from hot ash, like the forest's final blessings.

fog

KENOSIS

In sleep his infant mouth works in and out.
He is so new, his silk skin has not yet
been roughed by plane and wooden beam
nor, so far, has he had to deal with human doubt.

He is in a dream of nipple found,
of blue-white milk, of curving skin
and, pulsing in his ear, the inner throb
of a warm heart's repeated sound.

His only memories float from fluid space.
So new he has not pounded nails, hung a door,
broken bread, felt rebuff, bent to the lash,
wept for the sad heart of the human race.

STEPHANSDOM CATHEDRAL, VIENNA

*—"The catacombs tour has bones from
the plague and a room where
the intestines of royals lie in little jars."*

If I had to do the forensics, matching
the DNA, probing for pestilence or anomaly,
I'd wonder even more about the queen's
love life, whether the arranged marriage
with a foreigner bore fruit, or how deftly death
came. And the raptures of the royal cochleae
as they vibrated with Mozart,
even if I could detect them from the remains,
what would I grasp about
the life of royals in the 18th century?

Consider. Could you pluck with
the tweezers of your brain one tune,
like a fine blond hair from a nest of curls,
from all the messages crowding the air?

So much of life happens between the verses
of the psalms. When I got the tattoo, the pain
subsided as the image grew, the duet of flesh and ink
branding me for the ages with a flower-cross.
The likeness, on the skin of my right shoulder,
will someday toughen into leather. But why,
they'll speculate, did she do it? What
in her life was like a flower? A cross?

WALKWAY

My plane delayed, I wait the call to board—
a hiatus in the continuum, a lesson in patience,
the airport window at the gate like an eye
framing the almost soundless waves
of aircraft arriving, taking off.

The interior rhythm of the moving walkway—
a steel river, a continuous slither of hum,
interrupted every few seconds by
the announcement, The walkway is ending.
Please watch your step. Thank you.

Someone
is always being thanked by a machine
for not falling. Longing for a thank-you
to ease the bruises, I am carried along my corridor
toward a stumble onto the sill of heaven.

CAUNES, MINERVOIS

Under the hand it feels like satin,
as if we were caressing our own bodies.
Steps, mantels, windowsills, columns
carved of it, the marble of Caunes,
a rose-colored stone, its quartz inclusions
sometimes clouds, sometimes lightning.
Altar pieces. Tiles. Chips of crimson glow
from old walls, burning in arches that ache
with long bending and letting in light.
Sacred. Commonplace. Wherever we walk
a crackle underfoot, along with the ripe
figs of autumn, fallen and rotten, spurned
and spilling their pink inner flesh.

In the darkness of our *pension*
coughs of air batter the shutters.
The steady rush of rain falling. Storm
all night long, and in the morning
flagstones turned blood red and white,
raw as exposed flesh and bone, the wet
lying like skin on the marble.

CAMPING, CALIFORNIA COAST

Rain overnight, beading the tent fly stretched
taut over my head. In this nylon envelope I'm
shielded below by the thin skin of tarp
over an easy bed of redwood needles.

Low-hanging ocean fog takes the edge
off daylight, but when I stow my tent,
an earthy revelation: where no night rain could reach,
the sharp delineation between damp and dry ground—
dark with wet next to the pale dry dust—
is distinct as the knife edge that cleaves shadow
from sunshine when the fog clears.

Wanderers, for good or ill we leave our mark
wherever we land, whatever we touch.

THE YELLOW SQUASH

It seemed to grow with the light, the spring days
lengthening to summer, the single seed bursting
into beak and stalk, leaves like spread hands.
The forward thrusting end enlarged,
a curving length of neck growing to a bulbous
sphere, like a human head, it became
a personality, a member of the family.
All summer it swelled, a gold sun peering
through hairy green clouds until its immensity
made the sidewalk pedestrians gawk.

Detached, it waited in our kitchen. It felt
like homicide when we beheaded it for the potluck,
chopping the muscled neck into chunks to bake
with brown sugar, butter, and a mystery spice
we found in the drawer. (So succulent! Later
we made a generous soup with the leftovers.)
But the head, stranded for days on the counter,
wept large pale tears until the air
comforted it dry—the surface a patterned silk,
the ends of its fibers a circle of little stars.

LEAF, FALLEN

What held the browning leaf to its stem
so long—a link that lasted a summer's life time?
How ineluctably sap left the veins,

the spine curled. I hear again my mother's complaint
on each of her fifteen final years' visits from me,
I've lost a lot of ground this week,

as though ground were the one thing
valuable enough to cling to as the bones clot
and flesh loses mass and skin cells flake

along with the mind's most basic reminders.
Her friend had called her "a little brown bird."
She wore the russet color well but never sang.

Intractable, hanging on for nearly
a hundred years into an age that challenged
her understandings, duty was the word

that rallied her, not love, not living. And I,
her green leaf child, grew, and grew away, aching
always, for more than obligation, a need for richness that

offended her. In the cold's wither she finally let go,
let go of me. Clipped by a biting wind from a naked stem,
she fell to that ground she thought she'd lost.

ON READING GOD AS A POEM

The trail of connections is frail. I listen
for the oblique to become transparent,

straining to discern messages in
the deep silences between the calls of

a hoot owl on a moonless night.
Unfocused images try to crowd between

the words on some hidden script,
leaving me guessing. Conversation, the to

and fro of language, can never be a monolog.
But maybe I'm deaf. Maybe I should

partner mystery with my own silence. Or
is this a new language to be learned?

Struggling for meaning is like angling my view
to catch the glisten from a lump of coal

ready for burning, wondering about origins,
about carbon—its formation, its capacity

for warming a room, the life implicit in
some Mesozoic tree.

TO THE EDGE
for Madeleine L'Engle

Be with her now. She faces the ocean
of unknowing, losing the sense
of what her life has been, and soon

will be no longer as she knew it, as
we knew it with her. Lagging far behind,
we cannot join her on this nameless shore.

Knots in her bones, flesh flaccid, the skin
like paper, pigment gathering like ashes driven
by a random wind, a heart

that may still sing, interiorly—we cannot
know—have pulled her far ahead of us,
our pioneer.

As we embrace her, her inner eyes embrace
the universe. She recognizes heaven with its
innumerable stars—but not our faces.

Be with her now, as you have
sometimes been—a flare that blazes,
then dulls, leaving only a bright

blur in the memory. Hold her
in the mystery that no one can describe
but Lazarus, though he was dumb

and didn't speak of it. Fog has rolled in,
erasing definition at the edge. Walking
to meet it, she hopes soon to see

where the shore ends. She listens as
the ocean breathes in and out in waves.
She hears no other sound.

SUMMIT

In the tops of the cedars
ten crows are quarreling.
They do not believe in
conflict resolution. Now
they are flying off, glaring
at each other. Nothing
has been settled.

DREAM ON

When, just after waking, the last rags
of the dream plead to be pinned down
before they're gone, I'm left wondering,
was it all a kind of *cri de coeur?*

The scurry and scrim of sleep gave terror
a contour no daytime reason could construct
or deconstruct, feral and tangled, all bite
and vowel and colors I couldn't name.

A story line for a horror film. Flying, naked
from the waist, trying to hide. No shelter.
OK, a dream, but this was my life, hostage
to the raw psychedelics morphing

on the inside of the eyelid. Hoping that someone
can decode it, someone attentive to real
and surreal, to meaning, to me, caught there
praying, inside the dream, and no amen in sight.

NEW YORKER, DEC 7, 2009

A double spread: Two full-page photos stare—
Ahmadinejad opposite Obama. One face non-committal,
eyes narrowed, inscrutable as ink, the other,
a thinking man—ponders all the possibilities.

Overleaf—more portraits—Qaddafi's
rectangular, odd, implacable face across from Netanyahu,
(who'd ordered the photographer, "Make me
look good") and flip through the rest; a panoply
of world politics, a line-up of leaders putting
their best faces forward. Medvedev faces Yushenko,
Mugabe paired with Zuma, Zapatero across
from Erdogan, Berlusconi flirting with
Cristina Fernandes in her red leather jacket;
he's stroking her cheek with his eyes.

Now I've closed the magazine, page against page,
eyes to eyes, faces locked tight enough to sniff
each others' sweat, feel the rasp of beards. Will they
make nice in this strange privacy? Joined in a close
bond of slick with only slivers of air between, can they
ask what they really want to know? What do they whisper,
ear to ear? *I think my wife likes your wife. Off the record,
let me say…, Let's stay in touch about this. Make no mistake…
No sanctions, I promise. Did I hear you say 'Deal'?* And then
a sigh—*Now, if only I could believe you.…*

BREAKER

Any year of global upheaval, any typhooning,
quaking, heart-breaking, earth-and-mind shaking
year—it's then I remember how every spreading
fingerling of ocean inscribes a beach with its
unique story, each bead a survivor of hurricane
and tidal rip, of submarine violence, of sharks
and blood and the surface slicing of a thousand
boats' keels before its final relinquishment,
and a hint of expectation, like the long end
of the exhale before the next breath.

I remember. And now I try for reassurance,
now I assemble in myself knowledge
of what resolve it takes for a wave, spent,
flattened, idling, to re-gather itself into
a new spasm, an interior swelling up, a green crest
building itself in a boil of air and water
that overcomes its own lethargy and, energetic,
breaks, hurling its armfuls of shell and pearl onto
a fresh parchment of sand in a crescent of foam
that spreads higher with every tidal hour.

GOSSIP

It was as much about feeling duped
as being supplanted.

No cell phones or TV, but
the grapevine worked swiftly enough.

In his castle in Jerusalem,
Herod vented his frustration, cranky as

a squirrel ranting, head down
on the cedar trunk, tail quivering with rage

at territorial invasion. King? King?
What king? Not in my backyard!

While God was parking his throne
elsewhere.

THE PRAYER OF THE UPRIGHT

1

Near Lima, in a town where rain is scant,
the locals harvest fog, condensing it on nets
and wringing them like wet rags to water their fruit trees.

How to re-hydrate the drying world?
Might the vapor of fervent prayer contain
enough moisture to dampen the deserts?

2

Or my faith, might it swell, powerful as
imagination, so that God and I, persuaded, join
to preserve the floe under the endangered polar bear,
and consecrate the fresh crystals
thrusting like flowers around its edges?

3

How to be so soaked in the mist of Spirit
that what is wrung out of me, even in my outrage,
tastes like the dark juice of Eucharist,

a blessing on my adversaries. Lord, as I wait,
let your thoughts, like doves from a dovecote,
fly through some orifice into my heart.

4

But first, confession—the ripping out of
my knitted life back to the flawed stitches, as visible
to me as dead flies on the window sill. And

the refashioning, so that even my greetings at
the mail box down our street begin to heal my neighbor's
cynicism about the world, and you.

LOTHARIO

This plum blossom slut on her own pink
half shell—how can she not recall the sexual nosing
of each wanton bee, horny for honey,
legs dark and magnetic, fondling her,
dipping his wick into her plush, collecting
the heavy pollen trophies before visiting
the next, and the next lady, infecting each,
and off to the hive, humming as he goes?

THE TWO OF THEM

He's the black plug that fits no socket.
She's the small change that weights the pocket.

He's the exhaust in the atmosphere.
She's her own nightmare. She's the fear.

He's the cloud that yields no rain.
She's the narcotic that seeds the pain.

He's the dead dog that no one fed.
She's the needle that lost its thread.

He's the line without a hook.
He's the final gasp the drowned man took.

She's the rot at the heart of the oak.
She's the last word the patient spoke.

He's the trap without the cheese.
She's the hive deprived of bees.

He's a chimera, a heat mirage.
They're the gas fumes in their own garage.

ODD ANGEL

So what about this aberrant angel
in the De Lisle Psalter? 14C. No floating,
nothing beatific. The sharp edges of
uprighteousness, pinions aligned vertically—
straight and narrow, legalities
labeled with Latin, I try to make sense of them—
...*confessio*? features skeptical, a herald of disdain
at earthly impiety...*Vigilarium hominem*...
His hands splay at his sides:
"Now what?" a gesture of despair
at human transgression.

Okay, this one has six wings—what
does he think he is, a vision from Ezekiel?—
and bony feet treading a suspended sphere,
Orba misericordia... could be the earth or
a soccer ball, or some cherub's confiscated halo.

I must be fair; his own nimbus is flawless,
and every curly hair in place, with a scarf
knotted tastefully about his shoulders.
But a sneer crumples his face, *subractio odoratus...*
his pin-dot eyes glare left—a couple of acolytes
cracking jokes? If he's incarnating Scripture,
it must be one of the imprecatory psalms.
One more vigilante for original sin.

INDETERMINACY
(after Schrodinger)

Two tourists pass in a crowded bus.
The hairs on their bare arms touch,
for a moment meshing and warm,
then not, the door of the bus
already closed with a thud and a hiss,
a fragment in history, a swift
receding. That flash-point when
the future brushes against the past—
we notice it only after. Too late.
Now is already over; if
we stop to look, it's gone.

The heart in my chest—in bed
at midnight I shudder to its thump.
A-*gain*, it repeats, a-*gain*,
each iambic beat ending at
the instant of assertion. Showing up
only as one in a trail of alpha sparks
tracking through the corridor of
memory's cloud-chamber. Never
on my bus trip will that again
happen again.

O

O my sharp clove,
your dark nail probes my hand.
You stud my open palm
with poignancy, pinning me to
your final clench of cross-pain.

O my asparagus,
the cleansing sprinkle of your fern,
your up-greening from the ground,
your stalked asperity under the lemon sauce—
all waken me to resurrection.

O my avocado,
your vegetable comfort calls my name.
Teach me the colors of knowing. Within
your purpled leather rind disclose
your sumptuous spirit, your oil-hearted seed.

O my scarlet carnation,
your iron-fresh scent, and the torn,
spiked edges of your dying
out-flesh for me the colors
of God's blood, God's body.

NO, I'M NOT HILDEGARDE

I'm merely a floater in the eye of God,
a flake of his winnowed chaff. A twig
from the tree at whose root his ax is laid,
if you believe Luke, and I do. I am a wisp
of the fog that blinds my world today. A drop
from a leaking tap. An odd button. A blot.

I'm less than the smallest bone of St. Catherine's
withered fore-finger; in Sienna it's preserved
behind glass and I'm not. I'm a loose tooth.
A hesitation of wind. The lost coin never found.
A river wrinkle come and gone. An eyelash
found by an ant in the dust. A blink.

THE STONES, SPEAKING
Bellingham Cemetery

They thrust up like thumbs giving the OK sign.
But is it? These are place holders for identity, set in
frames of clean-cut, spring-green grass so radiant
it seems to hold some flicker, some blue flame
from those remains hidden, secret,
despite mortality, and the terror and damage
that hide below in bones and ashes.

Veterans. Ancestors. But here's one without a name—
Infant, Berman, Stillborn, May, 1898. And here,
with so brief a space between the dates,
Annie Curdy, 1931-1934. Something happened;
the three years over early, marked by a stone,
the period at the end of the sentence.

In Siena, St. Catherine's bony forefinger blessed us
from within a glass reliquary.
But inscriptions never tell the whole story. Sometimes
the lie is blatant—Devoted Father, Beloved Mother,
Dearly Missed—but on the sandstones the creeping lichen
eats away at euphemisms. Two hundred years
asleep in the old town's underground—
the myths and legends still bury their questions.

WHAT JESUS SAID

What Jesus said was
      what he did.
He said, be salt. Himself
      salt,
a zest seasons
      the world
      wherever he shakes
      his pungent crystal.

Salt-free signifies
      insipid,
      yet absolute salt is
      so sharp,
if all you eat is salt
      you die.

The words—
> they sting on the tongue—

The savor of action
> saves,

and deeds of salt
> preserve
> and purify.

Say it first, but then
> do it—

the salt, and then
> the savor.

CRUNCHING JESUS
John 6: 53-58

The communion bread is laid on my tongue
so gently. But I am ravenous; I want to gnaw
the whole loaf. We know already we are his body,
but taking in this crumb of the earth's generous
flesh, this sip of its given blood, presses Incarnation
into my flesh. As imagination takes in the symbol
and the substance we become more acutely
vessels filled with Christ. Even as we step away
from the altar and out the church door
we keep living the liturgy and the urge to Eat
and Drink. The wine burns still in my throat.
I have a pasty shred of bread stuck in my teeth. Oh,
how to feed the hunger and thirst of the world?

CROSSWAYS

In Purgatorio Dante
sees himself afloat on
the Arno, his body
wide-flung, buoyant
on the flooding river,
making of himself a
cross like the cross on his chest. The strangeness
of crisis, that sometimes allows a body to repeat
a familiar image of calamity met and overcome.
Fasting prayer for the hungry. Nakedness for the
destitute. A skin
pockmarked for
the sad diseased.
The poet asks the
poet in me, How
to live Christ in a
new skin, bearing
some part of the
earth's burdens, as
without boats we
drift, all together,
downstream.

NOW! ORDER YOUR PRE-PAID CREMATION!

I've seen the Kathmandu corpses,
garlanded with marigolds, burned
to a crisp, holy smoke sifting
across the river, censing the air for the tourists.
In Annapurna's narrow lap this valley,
chock full of bones, is too cramped
for burials. Instead, the dead are loaded onto
burn piles stacked with logs from the foothills,
now naked and eroding, pillaged for ceremony,
death gathering to itself more death
up the slow gradient of necessity.
Mourners chant. Mortality teaches
our ears, eyes, noses as the little boats of
skeletal ash and charcoal are launched,
freed from the funeral ghats,
to drift downstream.

Urged now to weigh the manner of
my final dispersal, I'm not
averse to incineration. But I confess
this foolish comfort: to lie beside my husband
in our grave—a double bed we chose together—
the full, aged remnant of the body he loved,
knowing heaven can pull together
from earth or urn, from bones or ashes,
whatever is needed for what's next.

ATTENDEZ!
The buildings of Languedoc

The buildings of Languedoc—tell about them. Tell
what words rose up like shards from the narrow streets.
Tell what the layers of centuries have done and how
the adjectives multiplied in the little towns of my mind—
cobbled, cornered, crumbling, drain-piped, pitted,
chipped, tiled, angled, stuccoed, mortared in sienna, taupe,
russet, ochre, slated, sooty, stained, gray, gray, derelict,
stone on rock under bleached, half-timbered wood,
brick-patched, cramped, motley, matted, mottled,
bleak, sun-warmed, weather-worn.

The multiples of windows, lenses of intimate life—
cracked, re-glazed, ivied, veined, silled, grime-sullied,
mullioned, intricate, stone-set, askew, open, lace-curtained,
barred, shuttered in indigo, peach, jade, robin-egg, apricot.

And the castles crowning the hills? Storied, moated,
draw-bridged, dungeoned. The walls crenellated, cloven,
carved, chiseled, sloping, slipping, blackened, blank,
grooved, arched, squared, split, molded, folded, gargoyled,
lichened, blotched, mossy, mildewed, stacked, slackened,
hollowed, caving, no longer embattled, reduced
to postcards in racks along the steep streets.

The churches—steepled, domed, Gothic, Roman,
iconed, groined, chapeled, gilded, stained-glassed,
dimmed, dusty, disused, deserted. The monasteries—
how thoroughly excavated, explored, researched,
dated, brochured, ragged, fallen, earthed,
bald as the monks of L'Abbaye de St. Pierre et St. Paul.
Besieged, fading in time like the Cathares. Like
the Cistercians of Villelongue near Montolieu, like
the martyrs—Armand, Luce, Audalde, Alexandre—
burned, decapitated, tortured, flesh flayed raw as
the blood-red marbles of Caunes Minervois. Lives built,
spent, spilled, splendid. Here words fail. All that comes
is what they were singing—Glory! Glory! Glory!

LaVergne, TN USA
14 October 2010
200834LV00004B/210/P